I Am Trustworthy

by Melissa Higgins

Consulting Editor: Gail Saunders-Smith, PhD

Content Consultant: Susan M. Swearer, PhD
Professor of School Psychology and Licensed
Psychologist; Co-Director, Bullying Research Network
University of Nebraska–Lincoln

CAPSTONE PRESS
a capstone imprint

Pebble Books are published by Capstone Press,
1710 Roe Crest Drive, North Mankato, Minnesota 56003
www.capstonepub.com

Library of Congress Cataloging-in-Publication Data
Higgins, Melissa, 1953–
I am trustworthy / by Melissa Higgins.
pages cm.—(Pebble books. I don't bully)
Summary: "Simple text and full color photographs describe how to be trustworthy, not a
bully"—Provided by publisher.
Includes bibliographical references and index.
Audience: Age 5-8.
Audience: K to grade 3.
ISBN 978-1-4765-4066-5 (library binding)
ISBN 978-1-4765-5170-8 (paperback.)
ISBN 978-1-4765-6035-9 (eBook PDF)
1. Trust—Juvenile literature. 2. Reliability—Juvenile literature. I. Title.
BJ1500.T78H54 2014
179'.9—dc23   2013029991

Note to Parents and Teachers

The I Don't Bully set supports national curriculum standards
for social studies related to people and cultures. This book
describes being trustworthy. The images support early
readers in understanding the text. The repetition of words
and phrases helps early readers learn new words. This book
also introduces early readers to subject-specific vocabulary
words, which are defined in the Glossary section. Early readers
may need assistance to read some words and to use the Table
of Contents, Glossary, Read More, Internet Sites, and Index
sections of the book.

Printed in the United States   6705

Table of Contents

Hy-Vee
just a bite

You can count

on me.

I'm trustworthy.

I don't bully!

come caught
can cat
dinosaurs
did do dog
Franklin
fly
go
have
and asleep
Ii Jj Kk Ll Mm Nn Oo Pp
I in it is
look like
my me new no not one
Qq Rr Ss Tt Uu Vv
ing
sh ch
said the to
too top
Story Elements
you yes Zz
6
Shapes

I play by the rules.
Kids who bully
take things
without permission.

I do my own work.
Kids who bully cheat
and ask other people
to cheat.

I tell the truth.
Kids who bully lie.
If I lied, people
would not trust me.

I keep my promises.
Kids who bully
only look out
for themselves.

I do my fair share.
Kids who bully
take credit for work
they haven't done.

CONCRETE
9 4
K8TER

I help my friends.
Kids who bully
don't stand up for
their friends.

I can keep secrets.
I only tell adults if
somebody could
get hurt. Bullies share
secrets just to be mean.